Contents

Food to live

Every living thing needs food to survive. Food gives animals and plants the energy they need to grow and stay healthy. Plants can make their own food using the energy from sunlight. Animals must eat plants or other animals. Other tiny creatures feed on dead animals and plants.

Links in the chain

Animals and plants are linked by the food they eat. Some animals eat plants for food. Other animals eat plant-eating animals. The links between all of the living things in one place are called food chains. Many food chains link up to make a food web.

Deserts are very hot places and only a few plants can survive there. Hardly any plant-eating animals live in deserts.

LIFE SCIENCE STORIES

Food Webs

Raintree is an imprint of Capstone Global Library Limited, a company incorporated in England and Wales having its registered office at 264 Banbury Road, Oxford OX2 7DY – Registered company number: 6695582

www.raintree.co.uk
myorders@raintree.co.uk

Produced for Raintree by Calcium
Edited by Sarah Eason and Harriet McGregor
Designed by Paul Myerscough and Geoff Ward
Picture research by Rachel Blount
Production by Victoria Fitzgerald
Originated by Capstone Global Library Limited © 2016
Printed and bound in China

ISBN 978 1 4747 1574 4 (hardback)
19 18 17 16 15
10 9 8 7 6 5 4 3 2 1

ISBN 978 1 4747 1580 5 (paperback)
20 19 18 17 16
10 9 8 7 6 5 4 3 2 1

British Library Cataloguing in Publication Data
A full catalogue record for this book is available from the British Library.

Acknowledgements
We would like to thank the following for permission to reproduce photographs: Shutterstock: N Almesjö 21, Mircea Bezergheanu 20c, Mario Bono 10, S.Borisov 4, S.Cooper Digital 20tr, CSLD 7, Rusty Dodson 25, Efendy 14, Emily Goodwin 9, Sandy Hedgepeth 16r, Jiang Hongyan 20bc, Igorsky 5, Iakov Kalinin 6, Cathy Keifer 11, Igor Kovalenko 17, D. Kucharski & K. Kucharska 15, 20bl, Dariusz Majgier 20br, DJ Mattaar 18, MP cz 29, Steve Oehlenschlager 27, Oksana Perkins 13, Dr. Morley Read 28, SergeyIT 16l, Dmitriy Shironosov 16c, Villiers Steyn 26, Alexey Stiop 22, Teerapun 12, Tjuktjuk 23, Visceralimage 20tl, 24, Marty Wakat 19, Alessandro Zocc 8.

Cover photographs reproduced with permission of: Shutterstock: Willyam Bradberry.

Some words are shown in bold, **like this**. You can find out what they mean by looking in the glossary.

True story

DINNERTIME

Some **reptiles** eat a huge meal and then do not eat again for many months. Giant snakes can swallow prey as big as a deer whole. They can then survive without another meal for up to two years!

Making food

Plants are called **producers** because they make their own food and provide food for other living things. Plants make food using energy from sunlight, water and **carbon dioxide**. This is called photosynthesis.

Plant-like producers

Plants are not the only living things to make their own food. Phytoplankton are tiny plant-like creatures that live in the oceans. They float near the surface of the water and make food for all the animals that live in the oceans, from enormous creatures such as humpback whales to tiny fish.

A chemical makes plant leaves green. It is this chemical that traps the energy from sunlight.

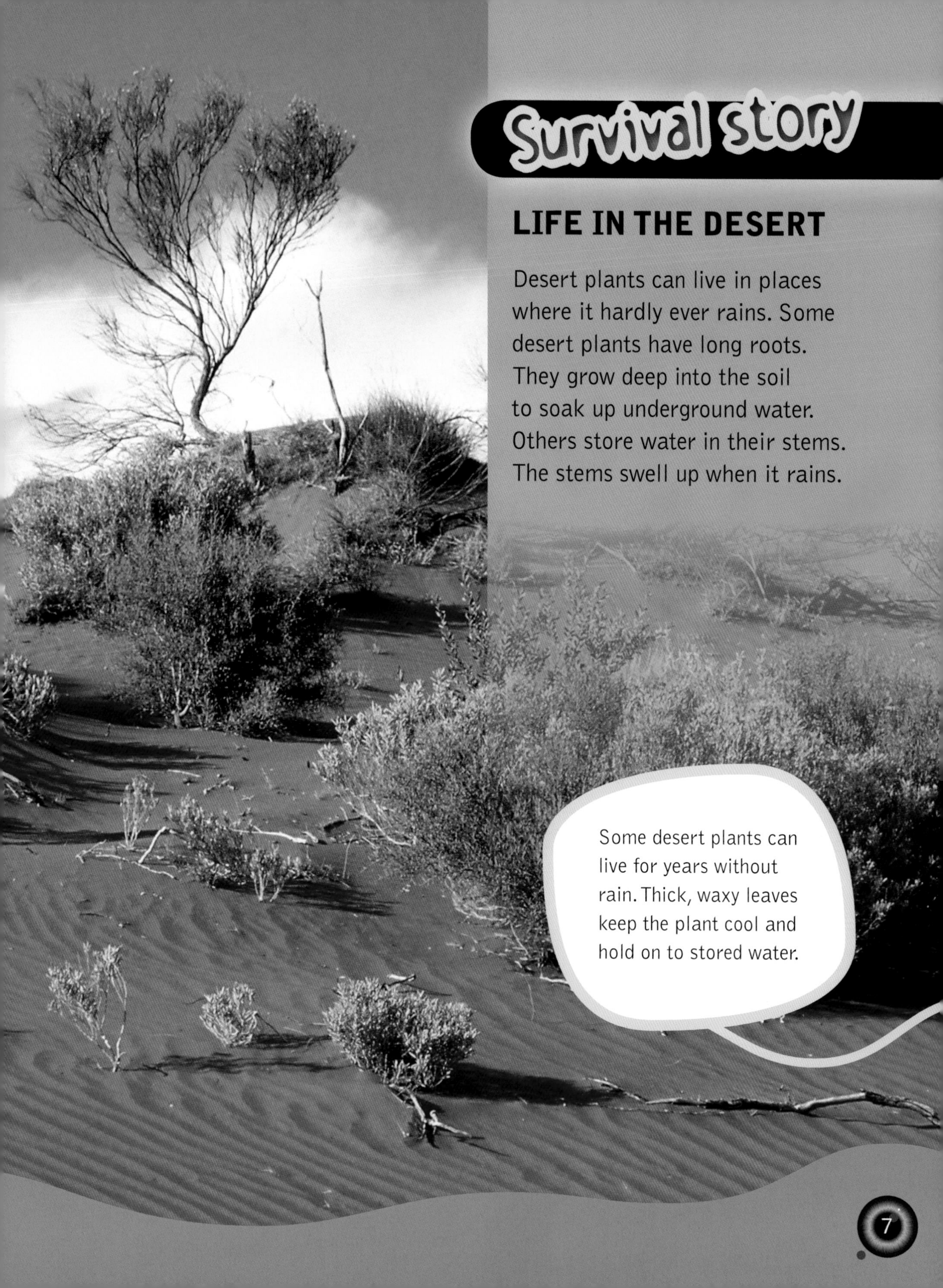

Survival story

LIFE IN THE DESERT

Desert plants can live in places where it hardly ever rains. Some desert plants have long roots. They grow deep into the soil to soak up underground water. Others store water in their stems. The stems swell up when it rains.

Some desert plants can live for years without rain. Thick, waxy leaves keep the plant cool and hold on to stored water.

Plant eaters

Animals that eat only plants are called **herbivores**. Some herbivores eat plant leaves, roots and stems. Others eat plant fruits and seeds. Still others suck up and drink plant juices called nectar and sap.

Grazers and browsers

Some animals, such as cattle and horses, are grazing herbivores. Grazers usually feed on grasses. They have wide, flat teeth that grind up plants. Other animals, such as antelope and giraffe, are browsing herbivores. Browsers pick off the leaves and juicy stems of tall plants.

This Barbary macaque is feeding fruit to its baby. Monkeys eat a lot of different plant foods, from fruits and leaves to roots and seeds.

True story

This bee is covered in pollen grains from the flower. It will carry them to other flowers. This process will make new plants grow.

FOOD FROM FLOWERS

Some flowering plants make a sweet food called nectar. Honeybees fly to the flowers, pick up the nectar and use it to make honey. The bees store honey in a hive and then eat it in the winter. People also eat the delicious honey that these bees make.

Meat eaters

Animals that eat other animals are called **carnivores**. These animals hunt and eat the bodies of other animals, including insects, fish or birds and their eggs. A few carnivores only eat meat. They include alligators and lions. Other carnivores also eat fruit and other plant parts.

Different meat eaters

When a carnivore hunts another animal it is called a **predator**. Some, such as wolves, are top predators, which means no other animal eats them. Others, such as vultures, are **scavengers**. They eat any dead animals that they find.

This leopard has caught an antelope. Leopards are dangerous predators because they can run quickly and climb trees.

This fly has landed on the leaves of a plant called a Venus Flytrap. The leaves snap shut to trap the fly. The plant then eats its **prey**.

True story

KILLER PLANTS

Plants need **nutrients** to live and grow. Most plants get nutrients from the soil. Carnivorous plants grow in places where the soil does not contain many nutrients. These plants get nutrients by trapping and eating small creatures.

Eating all types of food

Animals that eat both plants and other animals are called **omnivores**. Most humans are omnivores. We also need to eat fruit and vegetables to stay healthy. Many people eat meat from animals such as chickens, fish and cows. Some people choose not to eat meat.

Warm-blooded omnivores

Animals that have warm blood and fur are called mammals. They feed their babies with milk. Most adult mammals are omnivores. Wolves prefer meat but will eat plants to survive. Squirrels usually eat plants but will eat meat if they find it.

Skunks are omnivores. They eat berries, fruits, nuts, insects, frogs and even other small mammals such as mice.

True story

FEEDING FRENZY

Grizzly bears usually eat plants, but they will eat meat when it is around. In North America, fish called salmon return from the sea every summer and swim up rivers to lay their eggs. The grizzly bears stand in the water to catch and eat a lot of these fish.

Adult grizzly bears can eat up to 40 kilograms (90 pounds) of salmon in one day to fatten up for the cold winter ahead.

Break it down

Animals called **decomposers** eat food that no other animal will eat. They feed on waste and the rotting remains of dead animals and plants. These animals do an important job. They **recycle** any **nutrients** locked away inside the animal waste. They put the nutrients back into the soil so that other plants and animals can use them.

Tiny decomposers

Some decomposers are animals you can see, such as earthworms and millipedes. Others are so small you can only see them under a microscope. These tiny organisms are called **bacteria** and fungi.

Dung beetles lay their eggs inside balls of dung. The **larvae** inside the eggs grow into adults and eat their way out of the egg.

True story

EATING DIRT

Earthworms feed on the remains of dead animals and plants in the soil. The body of an earthworm is hollow, like a straw. The worm sucks up mud and takes in nutrients. The worm then squeezes out the mud at the other end of its body.

Food chains

Food chains tell us how different creatures use each other for food. Plants are at the bottom of most food chains. Plants are **producers**. They produce food for plant-eating animals, called **consumers**. In turn, these plant eaters are food for animal-eating consumers.

Different links

Plants are not always at the bottom of a food chain. A different food chain could start with animal waste, which is **recycled** by earthworms. A small bird, such as a sparrow, might then eat the worm. In turn, a large bird of prey such as a falcon, might then eat the sparrow.

Rabbits are one link in a food chain. Rabbits eat grass and other plants. **Predators** such as foxes eat the rabbits.

True story

TOP PREDATORS

Hunters such as polar bears, lions and large sharks are top predators. No animals can kill a top predator, but **decomposers** can feed on its body when it dies. They recycle the **nutrients** in the dead animal's body.

This bald eagle is a top predator. Bald eagles live near rivers or lakes in North America. They feed on fish, small mammals and birds.

Energy transfer

In any food chain, energy passes from one living thing to the next. For example, grass uses the energy in sunlight to make its own food. Some of this food energy passes to a rabbit when it munches on the grass. In turn, energy passes to a fox when it eats the rabbit.

Losing energy

Not all of the energy in grass that passes into the body of the rabbit is held there. Rabbits lose energy when they hop around. They also lose even more energy in their waste. The same thing happens when the fox eats the rabbit – the fox loses energy. Energy is lost at each step in the food chain.

These mackerel eat plankton and small sea creatures. Large hunters such as whales and dolphins then feed on the fish.

Survival story

FOOD BY NUMBERS

In any food chain, there is more food further down the chain. In a simple ocean food chain, dolphins eat fish and the fish eat plankton. Plankton is much smaller than the fish and the dolphin, but there is much more plankton than fish or dolphins.

For every dolphin, there are many more fish and a lot more plankton.

Linking the chains

Most animals are in more than one food chain. Many animals need to eat different foods to survive. A small woodland bird eats caterpillars and slugs. In turn, more than one **predator,** such as owls and snakes, eats the bird. The different food chains link up to form one food web.

Sparrows are consumers in woodland food webs. They eat seeds, worms and small insects. Birds of prey and wildcats eat sparrows.

Feeding map

Food webs are everywhere on Earth, from freezing polar lands to baking hot, dry deserts. Food webs map out what eats what in each place. They show all the **decomposers, producers** and **consumers** in every food chain.

A mouse is part of more than one food chain because it eats more than one type of food. The mouse is also an important meal for many other animals.

True story

FAST FOOD

Mice are very low down in a food chain. Almost every predator will eat a mouse if it is hungry, from cats and foxes to owls and snakes. That is why mice have so many babies – they need to keep up their numbers.

The hunters

Before a **predator** can eat another animal, it must catch it. Predators use amazing senses to find **prey**. Birds of prey have excellent eyesight and can spot a mouse from more than 3 kilometres (1.8 miles) above it. Owls have incredible hearing and can pick up the quietest movements of their prey.

Deadly weapons

Most predators use strength and speed to catch other animals. Some lie in wait and attack passing prey. Predators kill prey using deadly weapons such as sharp claws or a poisonous bite.

This tiger shark has an awesome sense of smell. It can pick up the scent of blood from many kilometres away.

Vipers have special senses that help them "see" the body heat of prey, such as mice.

True story

KILLER VENOM

Some snakes kill their prey with a deadly bite. They use fangs to inject **venom** into the prey's body. The venom is a poisonous liquid that kills the prey. The snake then swallows the victim whole.

The hunted

Just like **predators, prey** animals have super senses. They must look for, listen for and smell danger. If a predator is near, prey animals often hide by standing still. Some have body colours or patterns that blend in with their surroundings. This is called **camouflage**.

Fight or flight

Prey animals can still get away even if they are seen. Often they run, swim or fly away. Some animals puff up their bodies to warn off predators. Others use safety in numbers. Prey animals use claws, horns and teeth to fight off predators.

A bison can kill a wolf with a kick. Only a very hungry pack of wolves will try to kill an adult bison.

Survival story

COLOUR CHEATS

Most predators will not eat animals with brightly coloured skin. It usually means they are poisonous. Some animals are colour cheats. They copy the bright skin colour of poisonous animals. Predators think they are dangerous when they are not.

Balancing act

There is a fine balance between all the living things in a food web. Animals and plants fight for food and space. Sometimes, one animal lives while another dies. Any change to one animal in the chain will affect every other living thing in the food web.

Changing seasons

In the spring and summer, plant-eating animals eat shoots and fruit. These animals are food for **predators**. In the autumn and winter there is less plant food. Plant-eating animals may die, leaving less food for predators. Some predators die, too.

Cheetahs hunt antelopes and gazelles. They fight with leopards and lions for this type of food.

Survival story

ON THE MOVE

In winter, when there is little food to eat, some animals move to new places. This is called **migration**. Many birds fly south in the autumn. They migrate to warm places where there is more food. In spring, the birds return north to raise their babies.

Canada geese migrate south for the winter. They can cover more than 1,600 kilometres (1,000 miles) in just one day.

People pressure

Food webs are affected by people. Farmers grow **crops** to feed people. This destroys natural places where wild animals and plants live. Some farmers spray chemicals onto crops to protect them from **pests**. The chemicals not only kill the pests but other animals, too.

Chemical attack

Humans often cause accidents. Factories can leak chemicals into the air and ships spill oil into the sea. These chemicals kill wild animals and plants. When one animal or plant dies, the whole food web suffers. We need to protect animals and plants to keep food webs everywhere safe.

People have cleared large parts of the Amazon Rainforest. They cut down trees to grow crops and look for substances such as oil.

Survival story

TOO MANY FISH

Fish are an important source of food for people. However, some fishermen are catching too many fish too quickly. If too many of one type of fish are caught, they may die out. Other sea creatures that eat the fish may then die out.

Fishermen often use huge nets. The nets can also trap other sea creatures. This affects ocean food chains.

Glossary

bacteria tiny organism that is neither a plant nor an animal

camouflage body pattern or colour that helps an animal blend in with its surroundings

carbon dioxide gas found in air

carnivore animal that eats only meat

consumer living thing that eats other living things

crop plant that a farmer grows for food

decomposer animal that breaks down dead plants and animals

herbivore animal that eats only plants

larva baby of an animal such as an insect

migration movement of animals from place to place in order to find food or to have babies

nutrient substance living things need to grow and stay healthy

omnivore animal that eats both animals and plants

pest creature that damages crops

predator animal that hunts and eats other animals

prey animal that is eaten by other animals

producer living thing that makes food for other living things

recycle use again

reptile animal that is covered with a dry, scaly skin. A reptile is cold-blooded and must take in heat from outside its body.

scavenger animal that eats any dead animals it finds

venom poisonous liquid that an animal uses to kill another animal

Find out more

Books

Food Chains and Webs series, Angela Royston
(Heinemann Educational Books, 2014)

Food Chains and Webs (The Web of Life), Andrew Solway
(Raintree, 2013)

Food Relationships and Webs (Living Processes), Carol Ballard
(Wayland, 2015)

Websites

www.bbc.co.uk/bitesize/ks2/science/living_things/food_chains/play
Watch this animation to find the food chain's deadliest predator.

www.rspb.org.uk/discoverandenjoynature/families/children/play/foodchainchallenge.aspx
Try this game from the RSPB to see how much you know about food chains.

www.topmarks.co.uk/Flash.aspx?b=science/food_chains
Play this interactive quiz and then fit the woodland animals into the correct positions in a food web.

Index